EVEN THOUGH I MISS HOME

DAIKHO MANEHRII

INDIA • SINGAPORE • MALAYSIA

ISBN

PaperBack: 979-8-89322-285-2
HardCase: 979-8-89322-942-4

To the ones I love,
I give them all

Contents

Preface

Never have I ever thought I would bring out a collections of poems. It just came along as I develop an interest in jotting down my feelings on certain occasions. Over the course of time, I felt the need to explore my thoughts and hence the collection-Even Though I Miss Home. Even Though I Miss Home is a personal collection of poems drawn from life's experiences and thoughts recounted from varied adventures. In the initial poems, it reflects on the encounter with nature and day to day activities. *The Best Moments In Life, I Want To Dance With Those Fur, I Long To Feel It Again, Thou Art Nearer* and *The Harmless Buzz* categorically are committed to nature. As one flip through the following poems, it relates on mediocre life of a driver, football game and ethos about the road.

Further, as one dip into the collection, the version of poetry I envision is incorporated. Then, it moves on to poems dedicated to a friend, daddy, grandpa, teacher, and leader. Poems such as *Playing Fair Game of Creed* and *That Day* reflects on socio-political life of the day. Absurd thoughts are reproduce in the poems-*Walking Down The Stream, Dwelling Dark, As I Gaze The Following Fog* and *To The Wild Dreary*

West. In the poems *Into A Depth Of Infinity* and *Wave Well,* the notion about death is articulated.

In the later poems, most of them were devoted to the theme of love. It is mostly characterised by unrequited love, rejection, longings and reminiscences, a sense of loss, a state of despair and most of all-hope. *Even Though I Miss Home* and *While We Wait* were committed to those who have sacrificed their life in search of an identity. May this collection brings some stillness in your hearts.

1

The Best Moments In Life

The best moments in life
Come when you don't have a choice
You agitate, resent and hesitate
Because you're gonna trade
Your felicity and pride

Here, you cannot say 'No'
But nod and never dodge
You expect nothing propitious
And venture to fulfill entreat
Just to put in order

Then, when you least called for,
Everything turned sweet, and screen
Moments to share in million
The beauty, care and joy
Illuminate from nowhere

Amidst every outburst and resentment,
There's never a pain
That comes from compulsion,
It only yield moments
Worth appreciation and applause

2

I Want To Dance With Those Fur

I want to dance with those fur
Beside the bank
Counting those that disappears
Into the blue sky
The dream of sweet innocence

As I flatter with petals
Letting them oversee
Beyond the snowy abundance
I would let them tickle me
For a thousand times and more

I would then listen to their lullabies
Of swift, gentle and faint blew
Cuddle away in soft, fluffy breeze
Twining with the restrain autumn flow
And be like a gratified angel

The bruises in me would wrestle on
As long as I nestle in this serenity
Of delightful brisk memory
Traversing through edges
Recreating endless felicity and gaiety

3

I Long To Feel It Again

I long to feel it again
That place where I have to peddle
Up the hill, go round and round
The sloppy and curvy narrow path

My energy drains
And the weary air reaches my chord
Almost choking to sigh
But turn magical with the beauty

While it mesmerize my soul
My weariness just vanish
As though in a trance
Lost in the scene

A vale where serenity abounds
Of greeny hedges covering me

With just the harmless buzz
And the swift brook, I dance to be them

Then, took me to glance
Of how nature alone satiate
Swaying along with the hedges
Feeling a tease of heaven

4

Thou Art Nearer

None contemplate
On profound love tale
Until one venture
To this solitude vale

The zeal to appease
Blinded every adversity
As you yearn to jig with
Thy beauty of bliss

Dancing bamboos along the path
Will enshroud your en route
With musical breeze
Exalting from the gushing brook

Thou art nearer
To that serenity beat

As you hold on to your breath
To swallow what you see

In the vale thy soul smiles
Even to your weakest
Thou will long
To play the same fife.

5

The Harmless Buzz

The harmless buzz
Will hover all around
In the vale
To evoke your fleeting life
That thou art afar

The beautiful vale
Of welcoming smile
Yellow, white and pink faces
Pile with myriad green
Slake your fretting heart

Pushing all your melancholy
Into the breezy go cart
All your myopic vision
Is just a blink
To the vast greenery

By Thy crafty beauty
To Thy deft touch
Your wicked pride
Vanishes in a wink
As humility reign here

6

Till The Dead Of The Night

Gather round the bonfire
At the nearest *tokhu*
As the winter chill knock silently
And welcome untimely dusk

An elder tell of past ordeals
Of the forgotten heroics
The long wars and rituals
No longer visible

The moon stealthily light up
Flashing distinct ardent faces
Passionate to hearken more
Of the legends and adventures

While inviting each for a stroll
To stay abreast of the pursuits

Some folks tittle-tattle along the way
Till the dead of the night

The picturesque dwindle away
Putting the close afar
And bring the far nearer
Debased of the once merit mores

*(*__Tokhu__ - a sit-out mound traditionally build of stacking stones)*

7

The Fog Football

Never seen one, but heard in a distant
And the moment you get to see
Vague imagery, flash thought
Hover over on every wretched soul
Bringing to live the old thoughts
Where 'fog' helps win
The outright, chaste team.

The game came to a halt
As the visibility diminish
While the crowd swallow fog
Overflowing everywhere
Excitement crawls to contemplative note
To ponder, appreciate and skimp
The serenity, nature alone provide.

Man often obliterate the beauty
Offered in different silhouette
And indulge in annihilation
Beyond his ameliorating capacity
He only discern over the 'fog football'
That he was, he is and he will be human.

8

The Driver Raises His Hand

The driver raises his hand,
Smile, and show his rustic accord
To the one who just cross by
The other nod and smiles
And both drove happily away.

He is always focus onward
Pulling, pressing and balancing
At every ditch, turn, up and down hill.
He twist and risk his body
Just to keep the sitters' safe.

He does not bother colour
Nor any human divide
He simply wish less congestion
Whoever hop in reduces his time
And whoever step out relieves him.

He is another kin
Content with his duty
Patient and enduring
He has a family
Whom he love dearly.

9

I Feel Pain Too

I feel pain too
When you don't cover me
Leaving me with sores
As you roll in tonnes

I feel pain too
When you don't sweep me
Littering all around
And throw your wrath

I won't mind
Carrying you for hundreds
To your destinations
Revolving to the best

But if you let water flows
And dust reign over me

I will never last
To your dreams

When I am here
Make use of me
Clear me often
And tar me soon

10

My Neighbour Has Many Visitors

My neighbor has many visitors
And I don't know any of them
Nor do I know my neighbor
We stare and just walk away

Visitors come in one, two or three,
Some stay long while some don't
Some came out with wrapped items
While some with brief disabilities

Most come silently and soft,
Yet came out noisy and brazen at night
And when the whole village sleeps
Visitors play every fictional role

I don't have any resentment or relish
Towards my neighbor's visitors

Neither do I partake in their lousy fights
I contemplate in the equality of imperfections

Quench your thirst, laugh out loud
And make peace with yourself;
My neighbor has many visitors
And I am not lonely.

11

Be A Blessing

Lately I've realize
Every birth is a blessing
Showered with love
Long by all kindred

Cradle with love and care
Grew among many
Abound in grace and mercy
Every moment on

Fill with manifold gifts
Of love, joy and peace
Sent from above always
And live on with more blessing

You are blessed
Be a blessing to every soul;

Your one fall is not enough
To forget Thy love

Let your blessing make another
Realize Thy worth and
Shine together as we
Journey in this world.

12

I Owe As Much As I Would

For all that you've been
I won't be able to gratify your keen
With my proposed mortal gratitude
Nor with my kindest magnitude

Meeting me in my clumsy transition
Was like a prize worth not a dollar
Yet, you make it right by the collar
And let it dance in my own disposition

I may intrigue your esteem
With no design to team
Unable to fit in your reckoning
Failed miserably to your twining
And the list goes on
As far as to the moon

I am selfish-lost in my para
While with your aura

I've lots of fond memories and fun
Alive and kicking to the last run.
You've done your best you could
Now, I owe as much as I would.

(...for my friend, you've done your best)

13

Even Though I Miss Home

Even though I miss home
I can't come back anymore.
For it's been a long time
I've been to the jungle
And now, it feels like home

No one compels me
Nor anyone dupe me into
It's my duty and my identity.
I've been far from home
And I wish to be home

I starve and almost died
But the spirit never left me.
I eat every edible leaves
And when I see stars
It makes me feel home.

The war goes on
And I might not see my 'dream home'
Remember the rainbow on the flag
The blood I sacrificed today
Won't let my descent go to jungle again.

(*To my Grandpa H. Bosii)*

14

In A Muddle Warehouse

In a muddle warehouse
Sat down by the door
Overlooking the hanging *chayote*
And pale yellow walnuts
He begins in soft tone
About the many exploits

Move toward the old trunk
Lying for years
In dust, rusted and worn out
A good company for travel
In the bygone days
Took out collections
Of those written in his leisure
For posterity to retain
That were oral inherits

In between the chat
He smile, laugh and frown
That are now unseen
And cover in darkness
Leaves with a grin of glitter

15

We Only Dream Of You With Him

Born between the war and new nation
And blessed with all what man needs
Yet, you could never content
Until you begin to work in His vineyard,
You choose to serve Him alone.

Your every step, worth the count
And your every whisper, a reminder
To prepare oneself for next
Foremost in bringing our literary
Into every single hand, clear and loud.

Touched young and old alike
With your rhetoric and zeal do;
Everyone according to their need
You've marked yourself with letters
Which none would be able to replicate.

Now, the star has gone back to its place
And as we look up the sky
We'll vow to walk in your light
Though we no longer see your smile
We only dream of you with Him.

16

You're That Someone To Me

You're that someone to me
Who never gave up
In good times and gloomy days
Never getting weary of all the whine
Instead keep pushing forward
Ready to face any event;
Someone who keep family first
Compassionate, loving and sober

You're that someone to me
Who sacrifice all that is his
For me to grow stronger
Never put us in danger
While cheeringly steers the wheel
Of care, love and strong bond
Someone who never show his struggle
Resilient, sturdy and understanding

You're that someone to me
Whom I will always hold on
As my model, hero and man of nobility
Forever engraved in my heart

(…to Daddy, all love)

17

Into A Trunk

Sat beside a window
Leaning onward to a frame
Staring at the newly slice
To draw out the best

From one edge to the other
Musing if it slide
Would carve into sheets
Of higher value

While many tried
Some persists and turn champ
Toiling every bit of fear
For a seamless bear

Each day
Would try to pull and push

To let it soar higher
For an unknown destiny

Putting all that's worth
Into a trunk
Of willing minds
And drive on the best

18

With The Next Bell

Every morn
Wake up with a ray
Ponder on
And wait to say

For the eager minds
Each utter was wit
So, revise more than twice
To make no mistake

Walking down the aisle
A hundred or more
Ramping as the truest
For a purpose

With the next bell
Moves to another corner

With a varied pitch
To ignite again

For the newer faces
With familiar unity
Exhibit the scheme
Of seamless pioneering

19

I Write To Please My Heart

I write to please my heart
From my assorted emotions
Of love, pain and hope
Situating in style

It soothes my heart
And there is no stopping
As I keep positioning them

I am overwhelmed each day
How it releases me
Of the trauma, dilemma and uncertainty
To put up anew

I will keep up and urge every
To feel the flow
And please your soul

It's not late
When doors are open
To let you in
With a moment of worthy
To play with verse
And share your purge

20

It Is Not Idleness

It is no idleness
To read lengthy pieces
And comprehend the longevity
Of conscious delude

I am rather elated
Over small figures
Of magnificent magnitude
From a simple pundit

Far away, down and deep
Is my profound flow
Retreat with passionate attempt
Vilifying the known talk

Accord by none
Read by least number

Redefined by expertise
And relinquish for next

Towing of my own
Towards a dateless leap
Absurdity unwinding multiple wits
Drawing for a win-win

21

I Look Back To See Me Again

I look back to see me again
All that I have riddled and scored
Through dense pages of traits
From hillocks to another valley

Trading on an edge of dismissal
Steadily passed on to wide ranges
Making teeny weeny pace of hanker
For a few emergence of esse

To the west and to the north
Clinging to a sole definite design
Placed with sore and defiance
Rowing to a deeper depth of elucidation

Nearing a clarity of glittering beam
That keep resounding at every pause

Toiling for a bounty premium abound
In mysteries of sundry waves

Orchestrating in the order of merit
These I cannot rewind and rewrite
It remains as covet gleam ornament
To an incomer to refashion with time

22

Playing Fair Game Of Creed

The alarm light of the east
Thou art no more my yeast,
Now I only tune back
To the feed of the village
With my thumb quick mileage.

Tremulous over the loss
Halt the innocent's cause,
Demonstrates to the round
I've been always 'these wild'
And wow still to be styled.

The jewel valley of faith
Where knowledge has green saith,
Now tussles in the fire
With images, pain, and greed
Playing fair game of creed.

The dust rose to show might
Shrinks with blowing sight
Sliding down from the hills
Polluted in the lakes
And swim together when the flood shakes.

23

That Day

That day, the sun rises in the east
It settled with the beast
And new puppets were born
And crawl the same
To suit the flux.

That day, the ground was wet
It dried as jet
And mudslide on every mount,
And flood on every plain
Made both bargain and complain.

That day, the pawn made his way
It let the other pay
And nobody washed his linen
But let his black self-drown
To avenge his stab at the ritual.

That day, it was give and take
It began another hide and seek
And your wealth dwelt in rain
And your smile on paper
End with ant.

24

Walking Down The Stream

Walking down the stream
Counting the tiny leaves
I see lanes and blocks overcast
The one almost wrapped in ruby

Listening to the origin of man
Long ago, the life's adventure
Now drenched and dreaded with ego
Turning pale and stale

That's how it tick anew
Leaving dark encircle
Of merciless and penniless
Dark hollow calling

Where most don't want to utter
As it emit unpleasant

And create imageries of loss
Those that are forbidden

And I simply recall
The beauty and bounty life
Of more conscience
And shining rays of aura

25

Into A Depth Of Infinity

In disposition of 'lost'
Loneliness pricks in
Fill with desolate congregation
And lame decipher

Many take you for insanity
And peel you off
From the layers
You were born into

It is the puzzle of human
That takes you to farther lane
Of balanced world
From a disarray equity

The colorful frantic
And mesmerizing displays

Of continuity to paradise
Begin with 'lost'

This imminence
Let you demolish
The notoriety of lesser known
Into a depth of infinity

26

Wave Well

When thou art here in a phase
Leave no regret
Of thought that part ways
And cry for things
That matter less to you

Even if the luster of purity
Is stolen from afar
Let the storm wipe away
The stony paths

Just let your walk
Be a sheer trails of shadow
You can always
Wear along as a gown

The time for each
Is set and trimmed

While it slowly comes around
To tap you
Don't be surprised
Instead be swift to hop in
And wave well

27

Dwelling Dark

Where will those go?
Even if you live a hundred
The uncertainty
That flash over and over

Dwelling dark
In pages more than kindred;
Unpardonable iniquity
Over the hustle life

Paralyzed from within
To step up dauntless
Shambled with remorse
Pain and mislaid luster

For a daily dose
Of reposition to push

But never perpetual
Enough to slake

Argued self
A thousand or more
Inexplicably to set
As a normality to many

28

The Young Man Died Inside

The young man died inside
Unable to embed
In a dinky corner
For the fallen gem

It's illusion to recreate
That doesn't simulate
Or divulge the crashed pieces
To put in shape

The gift you hold on
Has long gone
Uprooting the longevity
Once patched and revived

The tricking time
Seem to present season

Of comfortable trail
And disposable moments

All through the bustling
Hot pursuit to denouement
It's only to deplete
With wavering wave of vanity

29

While All Those Moments Slowly Fade

While all those moments slowly fade
I keep recreating in vanity
Of lost hope, remorse and displeasure
Where nothing can fathom deeper
And I keep playing the next song
Unable to quench my exertion

Don't know why I keep listening
To all these soothing melodies
As though I can create the same again
Don't know why all these lyrics seem
To speak to me
As though I can requite

It feels like I just woke up to find sunset
In darkness, cold and silence engulfed me

Only wrestle for breath
And keep yearning for dawn

While my playlist has to last
Till the first ray of east
It strike straight to my heart
And never leave till it dies

30

I Lay Here Gazing

I lay here gazing empty dreams
Between the dark walls keeping alive
And my dream crumble down too
Still, I see bright light as I look up.

Yesterday, I was buzzing with the bees
Among beautiful flowers
Dancing to the tune of wind
And every day I locked it

I sought afar to secure for winter
And it's stolen by a passer-by
Now, I am left to be a wanderer
Compel to wait for next spring

Will the spring be near for me
Where I can be par with peers

Or is winter going to consummate me
While I shiver and shudder alone?

It's easy to finish off a comb
But require millions to build
Every outlay call for perseverance
And that's not what everyone deserve

31

I Am Just Another Deer

I am just another deer
Looking for spring
Running around every hill
On a dried cloudy winter

While my heart knows well
That it's vanity
And I knew it a thousand times
Yet, I keep musing over again and again

It is easier to keep silent
Than say a million in vacuum
I am being mean to self
And in many ways disagreed with fate

In a world of dreams and chaos
I keep hearing echoes

Of voiceless soothe
Pleading me to smile

Maybe I just have to keep
Whispering to the ears that doesn't hear
And speak back to self
To gratify solely

32

26 January

As I woke with the lousy hazy morn
Slowly got down to settle for a day
I could feel the chilling bite whispering
'It's not over yet' with groan

And while it refuses to warm me
I sneak peep only to find her
Step in from another entrant
To be locked in pursuit of ecstasy

Between the racing heart pulse
I could only sense the flavor of warmness
Dancing away in the room of mortals
Leaving the two rest on each other

While rhythmic choral troupe march
Drew away the attention of the neighbors

And in that climax of heat and exposition
The far echoing rhythm fade away slowly

Then, the whole rugged, shabby building shook
Awakening souls to a halt of silence
Just to discern-it's 26 January
And that's something not to be parted.

33

But, With Life

Betwixt the last scene witnessed alone
And reality unveiling from every lone
The whole world turns and shook me
With a glance of uncertainty
And playful absurdity

Turmoil of fear and darkness prevail
Paving every single breathe at peril
From the vast encircling rhythm
To the dungeon of agony and tear
Surely the avenger of sevenfold

Every step was a debate
And every hint was at the gate
The black hole opens up to swallow
The whole truth in a gulp
Only to feed greed.

I lie here deaf and dry
And open to any cry
Left in the wilderness
Never to be pleased by time
But, with life

34

Holding On To A Stranger

Holding on to a stranger
Measuring the tide of aisle
With cheers of chill in red
The rag just wink away

No longer than expected
The binge ceases to fling
And soon the new song toss
Over all the spilled bill

Familiar face in a hoarse tone
Just shook for a moment
Whispering the spring echo
Impede by diligent buzz

From a wreck wretched wrath
Buckle up the broken tie-in

For a mistook idiosyncrasy
Voyage away into Canaan city

He stands still branching on
Sewing up profuse yield
Fill with bliss and elation
Giving all indebtedness ever

35

From The Other Edge

It didn't go too fast
But surely not slow enough
To keep the two waiting to prove their love
It begins on a Sunday morning where
Truth pour out till to the moon

From the other edge
To the other alluring end
It was after three counts
The new season bud gives sour taste
Of uncertainty and occasional flatter

The broken trust
Lay inside the vessel
Only to fake around vanity
And wisdom found in each life
Both lies in the fathomless deep

The Pandora of love
Is not in me
Rather impediments will prove
The remains of coy
With the steady verses

36

Happy As You Are

I once found her abandoned
And it was love that raised
Molded and shaped her tough
And filled her void to the brim

While adding feathers to our love
Toiling and sacrificed enough
She runs into hiding without a clue
Tearing apart those built with tears

The hard-earned price
Has gone to some wrong loyalty
Leaving in shamble and disarray
That love's plan and wishes

Leaving by night in the dark
With marks of betrayal and deception

Inside this dungeon of lies
You've made me a clown

I am nobody to compel you
Nor somebody to sway
Ignore me as you do
And happy as you are

37

Searching For Love Here

Searching for a love here
That has long gone
Leaving me in gloom
And I am still stuck here

Hanging on my hopes
Trying to press the refresh button
Losing in those good memoir
Again and again

It has long left me
And I am just being brutal
Refusing to let go off my head
Still hoping if it was untrue

I feel like closer each day
And keep routing back

Simply lost in illusion
Unable to find a way out

A rough life going on
Tossing all over the woods
Wishing it to be over soon
Though holding so close

38

She Smiled At Me

She smiled at me,
Not to please me, but them
For they entail veneration
While time gave us to flatter and thither
With concealed thoughts of disquiet
It takes to another level
Of attachment every single tick.

A day came for the test of words
And it proved right and defeated
The impossible
The frequent stories of life's truth
Soon beginning to melt the stony heart
In a quest to solve the mystery
Of whether it was a wrong pick

It was time, who never stoop
Nor fail to provide enough
Of the many covet longing
The eventful longest journey
Ended in a small room full of love
Mesmerized by fearless wild dreams

39

That Taste

I was a loam to the onset,
A mulch to the languish trait
Enriching and clothing that pang
Covertly immolates in the proliferation.

In the dark, I was that distant star
Watching you repose in tranquility;
In the morn, I was that reverie ray
Absorb in your synthesis.

I was that drop to your full blossom
To be yank and rest in a vase
Expending the last scent
Of intimacy and validity

And faded to remind that was 'love'
Reincarnated as a wanderer;

Still longing to bind elsewhere
On the road to golden gate,

That taste
Will never corrode with any one thing
Nor melt with fire
But sealed and saved.

(...to the one you loved, you have given)

40

I Stare To Ease My Heart

I stare to ease my heart
As I forcibly try to erase
With those turbulent memories
The virtuous keep haunting me

Then, I meditate
And gone reclusive
And lost my sense of judgment
Only to see my empathy expanding

I hallucinate over my own fancies
Possibly presume I could patch
With some phenomenal craziness
Leading me haywire and frenzy

Oh! Woe to my chaotic heuristic advance
I can only scorn off my delusional elation

As I read, watched and was convinced
With some crafted fictional realities

The 'one' inexplicable question
Rafting on my skirmish brain
May persist till it perish
With multiple futile attempts

(...to all my passer-by, you did what is best)

41

I Saw Your Smile

I saw your smile
And my heart races
Knowing not what to do
To make you mine

I don't remember
How we met then
You were in my arms
And it was all tender

I smile, I dance, and I sing
Not because I'm good at
I just want to do it for you
Fulfilling our love

Lo! The flow was freaking scary
As you vanish in form

And propose to leave
How am I going to take this?

I don't really know
Where I am heading to
With the broken pieces
I'll keep mending till it last

42

I Carry On

When I try to write about you
Memories keep flashing
With one thought
About you in frame
Sweet, sorrow in explicit scheme

I went far to salvage thoughts
And try to be content
Yet, couldn't find any solace
Nor could I release anew
For, it was easier said

Days, months, and years walked by
And I couldn't understand a bit
It seem like the weirdest happen
In real life than on screen
And I keep sailing on

I carry on
This protracted relish
Trailing away my time
Still happy as ever
And that delights me

43

Down The Highway

When you know finally
You've to leave her
While you still live on
It's the hardest

Your tables are turned
And your hopes shattered
As it slowly kills you
In silent with prickly pain

Most painful to do
As the burn keeps boiling
Utter no sound
Poisoning the mind

You tried hard
To hold on

The grip of love
With all your finest regime

But, the desire to be reckless
Leaves you in silence
To be mended somewhere
Down the highway

44

With My Whole Heart

With my whole heart
I could not fill yours
Nor my soothing words
Make you happy ever

Every thought about you
Couldn't assure
How much I long to hear you
And see you every morn

My sincerest deeds
Couldn't convince you
Neither made you content
And left in the cold

Will you still hide
Your heart in the dark

Or quench my heart
When my heart is only for you

Will you still let it blow
Away to every corner
Wrap in some thin linen
To be wiped out

45

You Wane Into Somewhere

I found you shivered
Lost, and looking for a spring
So, I let you bloom in my garden
Gave fresh flowers everyday
And you dazzle so bright

You felt like the first ray of morn
Chasing away your bad dreams
There, I put my trust
That it won't break
In making each glow and prosper

Nay! As your feathers grew, it spreads
And when both are mellowing
You wane into somewhere
Obscure, unintelligible to me
Seeking for greener lea

I can't help
Letting you fly freely,
Soar higher as you wish
For I can't keep holding on
That doesn't find home in me.

46

I Keep Losing Again

Just woke up to find gloomy morn
Clearly echoing not to be torn
Over rush decision to tour
And see less of what's sour

Timeless for a few pieces of silver
To just let it deliver
On a daily account of shame
For caring less to be tame

It's just too shallow to parade
On a downhill ride for comrade
That's going to torment you ever
And leave you going crazier

Waving as though you're unbroken
Trying to score less of already sunken

Deep in the darkness of pale
Driving on the stinky stale

And they say
I keep losing again
For I am worth less prudent
To follies and insolents

47

I Swear

I swear I went on a wrong journey
Leaving traces of warmth
Sowing the goodness of love
On those trampled and trailed
Weary and yearn for calm

I swear I went into a deep dormant
Leaving all my worthiness
Playing with all colours of life
Trying to figure out a way
For those that requires more than me

I swear I went on to buy flowers
Leaving my only priced pride
Hallowing the tenderness of care
Drawing all conceal sublimity
Towards a strong tower of tranquility

I swear I went down into a deep gorge
Leaving all the armoury unlock
Hunting for a breezy spring
Gathering all that could leap
Onward to a battle not very daring

48

Leaving Aside

Leaving aside
Those beautiful dreams
Once aimed, focused and tried upon
You dare not let it go off sooner
And each day,
You confront a bit of discomfort
That pull you down inside
Leading to desperate moments

It's much deeper
Than what you see
And hear less about
The struggle that go unseen
And the pain that trigger unwittingly
For seasons

Of the little things
You put so much of detail
Now floating over
And stinking the heart
That was once filled
With truth, purity and serenity

49

When Though Hover

When though hover
Over vast meadow
Overlooking afar
And walk silently
Pausing each step,
Whirling into trance
Of the good things
Gone too soon

While the new routes are wide,
Open and calling
The keen to restart
Startled and stalled
For so long inside the den
Of fallacious priority
Deserted and renounced
Entail for devote spooning

The struggles are real
Refusing to die down
Despite of its withered leaves
And loosen roots

50

Am I Waiting?

Am I waiting for another Godot
Among these millennial
Whose half is void
And half-face covered?

Punch in, flip and scroll
Only to find apocalyptic unfold
Making it dreary
And uncertain openings

Will my wait worth
With all my lofty trust
And resolute persistence?
Only time tells the truth
As I am not giving up too soon
For some *jelibis* or ice-creams

I will play to the last dice
Driving through all the marred
And artistic dilapidation
Desisting all rebels
With freak imagery
And distort connote

51

My Own Puzzle

Who else are in?
And who else are kin?
I am in my own puzzle
Trying to find how to dazzle
Amidst these mysteries

If it was fate
Why does it have a date?
Crumbling every hope and wish
While the remnants are now a dish
But never part away

I tried solving everyday
Almost hitting the bay
Oh! It's nowhere close in real
It's forever in my heart sealed
Like I have to perfect

What's this so easy for some?
But so hard like building Rome
Will I ever solve?
And be dissolved
From this fear and uncanny

52

It's Not Pain

It's not pain
And I'm not hurt
It's not happiness either
And I am not happy
Somewhere in the dusk
And towards the dawn
Staring into the trance
I know no deception
Nor betrayal
When I am for countless

I am in the median
Of here to there
Overshadowed by the charm
Of welcoming hugs
In moments, it vanishes

Into film of less figure
With no injury
In a near and far
Pool of breathe
Sighing for a relish

53

I Keep Rubbing My Eyes

I keep rubbing my eyes
To have a clearer vision
From the many illusion
I am in less control
The fusion of devote

Frozen to the brim
Dwindle in and out
Of the trampled sore
Blink a little more
And still addle

I just want to ease
This reckless tease
That matters me so much
And float me to places
Beyond wild corners

Between the thin film
I blink again
And cast my fervor
To a distant lane
Where the crushed meet

54

I Tend A Wounded Bird

Once, I tend a wounded bird
Tamed and fed to her whims
And as the feathers are grown
I let it fly and dance free
And she flew far away
For so long in the wild

She came back with a wound again
And I begin to tend her again
This time, I have lost strength
I let her decipher the path
That life is cruel
When you dance too long in the rain

Time has few words to say
As life begins like a soup
It takes away the taste with cold
In pursuit of a dark prince

The old wounds will expire
And fiddle your heart a little more
So as to make you smile
Rowing to deeper menace

55

I Know

I know
I am into the woods
And wandered for too long
Even spring sprung slow here
And only dark clouds hover
Amidst the howling and growl

Showed me
The tale of ancient hermit
Clawing to survive
Enslaved by the warmth reminiscent
Of beauty throb and lone chirping
In silent melodies

The flurry race
And hoofing steps
Echoing from the gorge
Surface nearer to me

Inch by inch at every inhale
On a fairy flat fair
Shoo me down
To slumber in the meadow

56

Let It Remain In Our Hearts

Let it remain in our hearts
For I have waited every bit
And counted every second
To make you as mine

I pleased and pleaded you
To the farthest visible end
Risking and tearing my soul
All for a glowing smile

It was never enough and content
For a yearning heart
Always eyeing on a greener high
Yielding in painful losses

Miles away, and miles to go
When it keep rolling backward

And rest in a den
To be consumed by lust

For, once it was given
It's hard to retake
The very heart's impression
That would last a century or more

57

I Smile Each Time

I smile each time
Singing along every song
And dance to every rhythm
Following a step inside me

I played every game
Kicking hard to win
Smack more with a shout
And run like a trotting deer

But, I feel twinge now
Over a picture of us
With content smile
Hanging on a colorless frame

It was easy for you, not me
Shelling out one by one

Tearing page by page
Remnants from a coverless book

My visions are dim
And I hear less of us
But, the melody of bird's court
Makes me feel pain again

58

Have You Ever Feel This Warmth?

Have you ever feel this warmth?
Just like it's gonna propped out
Not painful, yet uneasy fussy
Making you think as blank mass
Over a broken memories back alive

I am going drowsy moody again
And I need to break this monotone
Of fair, smiling and twining sparks
Trying to pull me in level
Onto a hollow-fellow mind trick

I pace short and she shook me low
Rocking me spiny
From a silly prudence
Draining away my social scenic
To a town near skeletal picture

I am not sane over your seamless damn
Nor over your pitchy wily time luck
Wish me no more of your tricky dope
Pushing me wide nearby
Of emotions that burn a little

59

From A Why

From a why
If I have not had?
The flow of the stream
Of love, rejection and pain

Does it really matters
If your strength were suppressed?
That comes out
Of thoughts, ache and burn

When should I quit
If that were no discoursed?
The swollen hot tube
Of sweat, tears and blood

Will you not answer
If our existence was charged?

That basket full of solace
Now turn bleak, dreary and dark

Or should I torment on
If none can step on my size?
It's turbulent for a soul
That's innocent, tender and chaste

60

I Dreamt of Us

I always dreamt of us
Walking down the aisle
Holding our hands tight
Never wanting to leave each
And as though there is no end
To our happiness

Each day I want to love you more
And keep falling in love
With you over and over
I keep following my heart
As though we have a destiny
To our love

Just like the gushing river
Never returning back

To be swallowed by mighty ocean
Our love was strangled
Before it could sprout spring
Of unending rejoice
Now, I dearly miss every little thing
I once care and cherish

61

To A New Journey

To a new journey
Of less vibe and patience
I begin to row
Into a world of delight

It allures a bit
And sparkles for a while
Tingling away some rust
Coated with tears

Then, swiftly shift anew
To ponder on
The low melodies
Of dark renewal

I deepen my voice
And listen to the beat

Of the rising heat
On a new relight

To a new link
Of cherry blooms
And peachy color
I chip my solace

62

As I Gaze The Following Fog

As I gaze the following fog
I heard my own self
Whispering to an unknown
Obscure and mystifying at once
Slowly piercing into my head

Driven away to an unruly traffic
Of indelicate and smutty talk
I drool to suit my fetish
Snarling at every drift recreant
Unable to stand on its own

The engaging torment press on
To smother the mulling portrait
Of unbidden and abject misery
Stressing out all that is wily
And carved into some demigod

A tourney filled with meanness
Tempering the meek and demure
Devoid of all the heaps of applause
Straining down to a furrow low
To find a match of unholy rove

63

While We Wait

While we wait, some bloom, some rot
And some remain devoted to ideals
Of the long unsettled goal
Circling into every inch
That's always there and theirs

From the shining east to dense woodland
Young warriors are born to fend
Though the path seem perilous
And protracted with lost vision
An unwavering hope surrounds

Into the wild and deadliest field
Tread quietly with no fear
And ready to pounce on foe
Traversing through damn trenches
And sleep in deep shadowy covers

Even morn turns to night here
And had to keep crawling unkempt
To many perfidious expeditions
Yet, the zeal to liberate leads on
To a future more of self

64

To The Wild Dreary West

To the wild dreary west
Crown in misty red and snowy blue
I owe my heart an apology
Shovel out from filth and smoky film
That need less of an introduction

All to the sweet savoury address
Showered with relish and charm
I drove into a deep hollow
Of no end and wide illustration
Trying to add meaning after every pause

The glittering glamour of the dawn
Lift my limit to some purge
Yet, failed to calm my pearly insight
Trolled to an utmost prelude
Hesitant to dwell in an aura

It came to fore by silly summer song
Soothing the melting dried pie
Trembling for more delicacy
Not poise for any long remittance
I dig my own self for a tweet

www.ingramcontent.com/pod-product-compliance
Lightning Source LLC
LaVergne TN
LVHW091058150826
845673LV00002B/630

* 9 7 9 8 8 9 3 2 2 2 8 5 2 *